ONE MINUTE WISDOM

ONE MINUTE WISDOM

ANTHONY DE MELLO, S.J.

IMAGE BOOKS
Doubleday
NEW YORK
1988

Library of Congress Cataloging-in-Publication Data

De Mello, Anthony, 1931–1987
   One minute wisdom.

   Reprint. Originally published: Gujarat, India:
Gujarat Sahitya Prakash, © 1985.
   1. Spiritual life—Catholic authors. I. Title.
BX2350.2.D384   1986   242   85-29003
ISBN 0-385-23585-2
ISBN 0-385-24290-5 (pbk)

"Is there such a thing as One Minute Wisdom?"

"There certainly is," said the Master.

"But surely one minute is too brief?"

"It is fifty-nine seconds too long."

To his puzzled disciples the Master later
said, "How much time does it take to catch
sight of the moon?"

"Then why all these years of spiritual endeavor?"

"Opening one's eyes may take a lifetime.
Seeing is done in a flash."

The Master in these tales is not a single person. He is a Hindu Guru, a Zen Roshi, a Taoist Sage, a Jewish Rabbi, a Christian Monk, a Sufi Mystic. He is Lao-tzu and Socrates. Buddha and Jesus, Zarathustra and Mohammed. His teaching is found in the seventh century B.C. and the twentieth century A.D. His wisdom belongs to East and West alike. Do his historical antecedents really matter? History, after all, is the record of appearances, not Reality; of doctrines, not of Silence.

It will only take a minute to read each of the anecdotes that follow. You will probably find the Master's language baffling, exasperating, even downright meaningless. This, alas, is not an easy book! It was written not to instruct but to Awaken. Concealed within its pages (not in the printed words, not even in the tales, but in its spirit, its mood, its atmosphere) is a Wisdom which cannot be conveyed in human speech. As you read the printed page and struggle with the Master's cryptic language, it is possible that you will unwittingly chance upon the Silent Teaching that lurks within the book, and be Awakened—and transformed. This is what Wisdom means: To be changed without the slightest effort on your part, to be transformed, believe it or not, merely by waking to the reality that is not words, that lies beyond the reach of words.

If you are fortunate enough to be Awakened thus, you will know why the finest language is the one that is not spoken, the finest action is the one that is not done and the finest change is the one that is not willed.

Caution·   *Take the tales in tiny doses—one or two at a time. An overdose will lower their potency.*

MIRACLES

A man traversed land and sea to check
for himself the Master's extraordinary fame.

"What miracles has your Master worked?"
he said to a disciple.

"Well, there are miracles and miracles.
In your land it is regarded as a miracle if
God does someone's will. In our country it
is regarded as a miracle if someone does
the will of God."

ADULTHOOD

To a disciple who was always at his prayers the Master said, "When will you stop leaning on God and stand on your own two feet?"

The disciple was astonished. "But you are the one who taught us to look on God as Father!"

"When will you learn that a father isn't someone you can lean on but someone who rids you of your tendency to lean?"

SENSITIVITY

"How shall I experience my oneness
with creation?"

"By listening," said the Master.

"And how am I to listen?"

"Become an ear that gives heed to
every single thing the universe
is saying. The moment you hear
something you yourself are saying,
stop."

ABSURDITY

The Master kept scraping a brick against the
floor of the room where his disciple sat in
meditation.

At first the disciple was content, taking this to be
a test of his powers of concentration. But when
the sound became unbearable he burst out,
"What on earth are you doing? Can't you
see I am in meditation?"

"I'm polishing this brick to make a mirror
out of it," said the Master.

"You're crazy! How can you make a mirror
out of a brick?"

"No crazier than you! How can you make a
meditator out of the self?"

CLARITY

"Don't look for God," the Master said.
"Just look—and all will be revealed."

"But how is one to look?"

"Each time you look at anything, see
only what is there and nothing else."

The disciples were bewildered, so the
Master made it simpler: "For instance: When
you look at the moon, see the moon and
nothing else."

"What else could one see except the moon
when one looks at the moon?"

"A hungry person could see a ball of
cheese. A lover, the face of his beloved."

RELIGION

The governor on his travels stepped in to pay homage to the Master.

"Affairs of state leave me no time for lengthy dissertations," he said. "Could you put the essence of religion into a paragraph or two for a busy man like me?"

"I shall put it into a single word for the benefit of your highness."

"Incredible! What is that unusual word?"

"Silence."

"And what is the way to Silence?"

"Meditation."

"And what, may I ask, is meditation?"

"Silence."

SPIRITUALITY

Even though it was the Master's Day of Silence,
a traveler begged for a word of wisdom that
would guide him through life's journey.

The Master nodded affably, took a sheet of
paper and wrote a single word on it: "Awareness."

The visitor was perplexed. "That's too brief.
Would you please expand on it a bit?"

The Master took the paper back and wrote:
"Awareness, awareness, awareness."

"But what do these words *mean?*" said the
stranger helplessly.

The Master reached out for the paper and
wrote: "Awareness, awareness, awareness
means AWARENESS."

VIGILANCE

"Is there anything I can do to make myself Enlightened?"

"As little as you can do to make the sun rise in the morning."

"Then of what use are the spiritual exercises you prescribe?"

"To make sure you are not asleep when the sun begins to rise."

PRESENCE

"Where shall I look for Enlightenment?"

"Here."

"When will it happen?"

"It is happening right now."

"Then why don't I experience it?"

"Because you do not look."

"What should I look for?"

"Nothing. Just look."

"At what?"

"Anything your eyes alight upon."

"Must I look in a special kind of way?"

"No. The ordinary way will do."

"But don't I always look the ordinary way?"

"No."

"Whyever not?"

"Because to look you must be here. You're mostly somewhere else."

DEPTH

Said the Master to the businessman:
"As the fish perishes on dry land, so
you perish when you get entangled in
the world. The fish must return to the
water—you must return to solitude."

The businessman was aghast. "Must I give
up my business and go into a monastery?"

"No no. Hold on to your business
and go into your heart."

INTERIORITY

The disciple asked for a word of wisdom.

Said the Master, "Go sit within your
cell and your cell will teach you wisdom."

"But I have no cell. I am no monk."

"Of course you have a cell. Look within."

CHARISM

The disciple was a Jew. "What good work shall I do to be acceptable to God?"

"How should I know?" said the Master. "Your Bible says that Abraham practiced hospitality and God was with him. Elias loved to pray and God was with him. David ruled a kingdom and God was with him too."

"Is there some way I can find my own allotted work?"

"Yes. Search for the deepest inclination of your heart and follow it."

HARMONY

For all his traditional ways, the Master
had scant respect for rules and for traditions.

A quarrel once broke out between a disciple
and his daughter because the man kept insisting
that the girl conform to the rules of their
religion in the choice of her prospective husband.

The Master openly sided with the girl.

When the disciple expressed his surprise
that a holy man would do this, the Master
said, "You must understand that life is
just like music, which is made more by feeling
and by instinct than by rules."

UNDERSTANDING

"How shall I get the grace of never judging
my neighbor?"

"Through prayer."

"Then why have I not found it yet?"

"Because you haven't prayed in the right
place."

"Where is that?"

"In the heart of God."

"And how do I get there?"

"Understand that anyone who sins does not
know what he is doing and deserves to be forgiven."

ILLUSION

"How shall I attain Eternal Life?"

"Eternal Life is now. Come into the present."

"But I *am* in the present now, am I not?"

"No."

"Why not?"

"Because you haven't dropped your past."

"Why should I drop my past? Not all of it
is bad."

"The past is to be dropped not because it
is bad but because it is dead."

PROPHECY

"I wish to become a teacher of the Truth."

"Are you prepared to be ridiculed, ignored and starving till you are forty-five?"

"I am. But tell me: What will happen after I am forty-five?"

"You will have grown accustomed to it."

IMPROVEMENT

A young man squandered all his inherited wealth. As generally happens in such cases, the moment he was penniless he found that he was friendless too.

At his wit's end, he sought the Master out and said, "What is to become of me? I have no money and no friends."

"Don't worry, son. Mark my words: All will be well with you again."

Hope shone in the young man's eyes. "Will I be rich again?"

"No. You will get used to being penniless and lonely."

PRAGMATISM

The disciple was planning her wedding banquet
and declared that out of love for the poor she
had gotten her family to go against convention by
seating the poor guests at the head of the table
and the rich guests at the door.

She looked into the Master's eyes, expecting
his approval.

The Master stopped to think, then said, "That
would be most unfortunate, my dear. No one
would enjoy the wedding. Your family would be
embarrassed, your rich guests insulted and
your poor guests hungry, for they would be too
self-conscious at the head of the table to
eat their fill."

IGNORANCE

The young disciple was such a prodigy that scholars from everywhere sought his advice and marveled at his learning.

When the governor was looking for an adviser, he came to the Master and said, "Tell me, is it true that the young man knows as much as they say he does?"

"Truth to tell," said the Master wryly, "the fellow reads so much I don't see how he could ever find the time to know anything."

MYTHS

The Master gave his teaching in parables and
stories, which his disciples listened to with
pleasure—and occasional frustration, for
they longed for something deeper.

The Master was unmoved. To all their objections
he would say, "You have yet to understand, my
dears, that the shortest distance between a
human being and Truth is a story."

Another time he said, "Do not despise the
story. A lost gold coin is found by means of
a penny candle; the deepest truth is found
by means of a simple story."

HAPPINESS

"I am in desperate need of help—or I'll go crazy. We're living in a single room—my wife, my children and my in-laws. So our nerves are on edge, we yell and scream at one another. The room is a hell."

"Do you promise to do whatever I tell you?" said the Master gravely.

"I swear I shall do anything."

"Very well. How many animals do you have?"

"A cow, a goat and six chickens."

"Take them all into the room with you. Then come back after a week."

The disciple was appalled. But he had promised to obey! So he took the animals in. A week later he came back, a pitiable figure, moaning, "I'm a nervous wreck. The dirt! The stench! The noise! We're all on the verge of madness!"

"Go back," said the Master, "and put the animals out."

The man ran all the way home. And came back the following day, his eyes sparkling with joy. "How sweet life is! The animals are out. The home is a Paradise—so quiet and clean and roomy!"

MEDITATION

A disciple fell asleep and dreamed that he had entered Paradise. To his astonishment he found his Master and the other disciples sitting there, absorbed in meditation.

"Is this the reward of Paradise?" he cried. "Why, this is exactly the sort of thing we did on earth!"

He heard a Voice exclaim, "Fool! You think those meditators are in Paradise? It is just the opposite—Paradise is in the meditators."

REALISM

A gambler once said to the Master, "I was caught cheating at cards yesterday, so my partners beat me up and threw me out of the window. What would you advise me to do?"

The Master looked straight through the man and said, "If I were you, from now on I would play on the ground floor."

This startled the disciples. "Why didn't you tell him to stop gambling?" they demanded.

"Because I knew he wouldn't," was the Master's simple and sagacious explanation.

SPEECH

The disciple couldn't wait to
tell the Master the rumor he
had heard in the marketplace.

"Wait a minute," said the
Master. "What you plan to tell us,
is it true?"

"I don't think it is."

"Is it useful?"

"No, it isn't."

"Is it funny?"

"No."

"Then why should we be hearing it?"

SPIRITUAL RELIEF

The Master held that no words were bad if they were used in an appropriate context.

When he was told that one of his disciples was given to swearing, he remarked, "Profanity has been known to offer spiritual relief denied to prayer."

GOSSIP

A disciple confessed his bad habit of repeating gossip.

Said the Master wickedly, "Repeating it wouldn't be so bad if you did not improve on it."

MOTION

To the disciples who were always asking for words of wisdom the Master said, "Wisdom is not expressed in words. It reveals itself in action."

But when he saw them plunge headlong into activity, he laughed aloud and said, "That isn't action. That's motion."

IMPRISONMENT

"You are so proud of your intelligence," said the Master to a disciple. "You are like the condemned man who is proud of the vastness of his prison cell."

IDENTITY

"How does one seek union with God?"

"The harder you seek, the more distance you create between Him and you."

"So what does one do about the distance?"

"Understand that it isn't there."

"Does that mean that God and I are one?"

"Not one. Not two."

"How is that possible?"

"The sun and its light, the ocean and the wave, the singer and his song—not one. Not two."

DISCRIMINATION

Said the jilted lover, "I have burned my fingers once. I shall never fall in love again."

Said the Master, "You are like the cat who, having burned itself from sitting on a stove, refused to sit again."

MECHANICALNESS

The Master once asked his disciples which
was more important: wisdom or action.

The disciples were unanimous: "Action,
of course. Of what use is wisdom that does
not show itself in action?"

Said the Master, "And of what use is action
that proceeds from an unenlightened heart?"

WORSHIP

To the disciple who was overly respectful
the Master said, "Light is reflected on a
wall. Why venerate the wall? Be attentive
to the light."

AVOIDANCE

A tourist looking at the portraits of former Masters in the temple said, "Are there any Masters left on earth?"

"There is one," said the guide. The tourist solicited an audience with the Master and started with the question: "Where are the great Masters to be found today?"

"Traveler!" cried the Master.

"Sir!" the tourist answered reverently.

"Where are YOU?"

DESTINY

To a woman who complained about her destiny the Master said, "It is you who make your destiny."

"But surely I am not responsible for being born a woman?"

"Being born a woman isn't destiny. That is fate. Destiny is how you accept your womanhood and what you make of it."

REBIRTH

"Make a clean break with your past and you will be Enlightened," said the Master.

"I am doing that by degrees."

"Growth is achieved by degrees. Enlightenment is instantaneous."

Later he said, "Take the leap! You cannot cross a chasm in little jumps."

DREAMS

"When will I be Enlightened?"

"When you *see,*" the Master said.

"See what?"

"Trees and flowers and moon and stars."

"But I see these every day."

"No. What you see is paper trees, paper flowers, paper moons and paper stars. For you live not in reality but in your words and thoughts."

And for good measure, he added gently, "You live a paper life, alas, and will die a paper death."

TRANSFORMATION

To a disciple who was forever complaining about others the Master said, "If it is peace you want, seek to change yourself, not other people. It is easier to protect your feet with slippers than to carpet the whole of the earth."

REACTION

The Master was asked by what criterion he selected his disciples.

He said, "I act in a submissive and humble manner. Those who become haughty in response to my humility I immediately reject. Those who revere me because of my humble demeanor I reject with equal speed."

PHILOSOPHY

Before the visitor embarked upon discipleship, he wanted assurance from the Master.

"Can you teach me the goal of human life?"

"I cannot."

"Or at least its meaning?"

"I cannot."

"Can you indicate to me the nature of death and of life beyond the grave?"

"I cannot."

The visitor walked away in scorn. The disciples were dismayed that their Master had been shown up in a poor light.

Said the Master soothingly, "Of what is it to comprehend life's nature and life's meaning if you have never tasted it? I'd rather you ate your pudding than speculated on it."

DISCIPLESHIP

To a visitor who asked to become his disciple the Master said, "You may live with me, but don't become my follower."

"Whom, then, shall I follow?"

"No one. The day you follow someone you cease to follow Truth."

BLINDNESS

"May I become your disciple?"

"You are only a disciple because your eyes are closed. The day you open them you will see there is nothing you can learn from me or anyone."

"What then is a Master for?"

"To make you see the uselessness of having one."

MEDIATION

"Why do you need a Master?" asked a
visitor of one of the disciples.

"If water must be heated, it needs a
vessel as an intermediary between the
fire and itself," was the answer.

SURVIVAL

Each day the disciple would ask the same
question: "How shall I find God?"

And each day he would get the same mysterious
answer: "Through desire."

"But I desire God with all my heart, don't
I? Then why have I not found him?"

One day the Master happened to be bathing in
the river with the disciple. He pushed the
man's head underwater and held it there while
the poor fellow struggled desperately to break loose.

Next day it was the Master who began the
conversation. "Why did you struggle so
when I held your head under water?"

"Because I was gasping for air."

"When you are given the grace to gasp for God
the way you gasped for air, you will have found him."

ESCAPE

The Master became a legend in his lifetime.
It was said that God once sought his advice:
"I want to play a game of hide-and-seek with
humankind. I've asked my Angels what the best
place is to hide in. Some say the depth of
the ocean. Others the top of the highest
mountain. Others still the far side of the
moon or a distant star. What do you suggest?"

Said the Master, "Hide in the human heart. That's
the last place they will think of!"

NONVIOLENCE

A snake in the village had bitten so many
people that few dared go into the fields.
Such was the Master's holiness that he was
said to have tamed the snake and persuaded
it to practice the discipline of nonviolence.

It did not take long for the villagers to
discover that the snake had become harmless.
They took to hurling stones at it and dragging
it about by its tail.

The badly battered snake crawled into the
Master's house one night to complain. Said the
Master, "Friend, you've stopped frightening
people—that's bad!"

"But it was you who taught me to practice
the discipline of nonviolence!"

"I told you to stop hurting—not to stop
hissing!"

DISTRACTION

A debate raged among the disciples as to
which was the most difficult task of all:
To write down what God revealed as Scripture,
to understand what God had revealed in
Scripture or to explain Scripture to others
after one had understood it.

Said the Master, when asked his opinion,
"I know of a more difficult task than any
of those three."

"What is it?"

"Trying to get you blockheads to see
reality as it is."

HOMECOMING

"There are three stages in one's spiritual development," said the Master. "The carnal, the spiritual and the divine."

"What is the carnal stage?" asked the eager disciples.

"That's the stage when trees are seen as trees and mountains as mountains."

"And the spiritual?"

"That's when one looks more deeply into things—then trees are no longer trees and mountains no longer mountains."

"And the divine?"

"Ah, that's Enlightenment," said the Master with a chuckle, "when trees become trees again and mountains, mountains."

STERILITY

The Master had no use at all
for scholarly discourses. He
called them "pearls of wisdom."

"But if they are pearls, why
do you scorn them?" said
the disciples.

"Have you ever known pearls
to grow when planted in a
field?" was the reply.

SPEECHLESSNESS

"Of what use is your learning and your
devotions? Does a donkey become wise
through living in a library or a mouse
acquire holiness from living in a church?"

"What is it, then, we need?"

"A heart."

"How does one get that?"

The Master would not say. What could
he say that they wouldn't turn into
a subject to be learned or an object
of devotion?

ARRIVAL

"Is the path to Enlightenment
difficult or easy?"

"It is neither."

"Why not?"

"Because it isn't there."

"Then how does one travel
to the goal?"

"One doesn't. This is a
journey without distance.
Stop traveling and you arrive."

EVOLUTION

The following day the Master said,
"It is, alas, easier to travel
than to stop."

The disciples demanded to know why.

"Because as long as you travel to
a goal, you can hold on to a dream.
When you stop, you face reality."

"How shall we ever change if we
have no goals or dreams?" asked
the mystified disciples.

"Change that is real is change
that is not willed. Face reality
and unwilled change will happen."

UNCONSCIOUSNESS

"Where can I find God?"

"He's right in front
of you."

"Then why do I fail
to see him?"

"Why does the drunkard
fail to see his home?"

Later the Master said,
"Find out what it is that
makes you drunk. To see
you must be sober."

RESPONSIBILITY

The Master set out on a journey with one
of his disciples. At the outskirts of the
village they ran into the governor, who,
mistakenly thinking they had come to welcome
him to the village, said, "You really didn't
have to go to all this trouble to welcome me."

"You are mistaken, your highness," said
the disciple. "We're on a journey, but had
we known you were coming we would have gone
to even greater pains to welcome you."

The Master did not say a word. Toward evening
he said, "Did you have to tell him that
we had not come to welcome him? Did you see
how foolish he felt?"

"But had we not told him the truth, would
we not have been guilty of deceiving him?"

"We would not have deceived him at all,"
said the Master. "He would have deceived himself."

ATHEISM

To the disciples' delight the Master said
he wanted a new shirt for his birthday. The
finest cloth was bought. The village tailor
came in to have the Master measured, and
promised, by the will of God, to make the
shirt within a week.

A week went by and a disciple was dispatched
to the tailor while the Master excitedly waited
for his shirt. Said the tailor, "There has been
a slight delay. But, by the will of God, it will
be ready by tomorrow."

Next day the tailor said, "I'm sorry it
isn't done. Try again tomorrow and, if God
so wills, it will certainly be ready."

The following day the Master said, "Ask
him how long it will take if he keeps
God out of it."

PROJECTION

"Why is everyone here so
happy except me?"

"Because they have learned
to see goodness and beauty
everywhere," said the Master.

"Why don't I see goodness
and beauty everywhere?"

"Because you cannot see
outside of you what you
fail to see inside."

PRIORITIES

According to legend, God sent an Angel to the
Master with this message: "Ask for a million
years of life and they will be given you. Or
a million million. How long do you wish to live?"

"Eighty years," said the Master without the
slightest hesitation.

The disciples were dismayed. "But, Master, if
you lived for a million years, think how many
generations would profit by your wisdom."

"If I lived for a million years, people would
be more intent on lengthening their lives
than on cultivating wisdom."

DEPENDENCE

To a disciple who depended overmuch on
books the Master said:

"A man came to the market with a shopping
list and lost it. When to his great joy he found
it again, he read it eagerly, held on to it till
he had done his shopping—then threw it away as
a useless scrap of paper."

EFFORTLESSNESS

To a man who hesitated to embark
on the spiritual quest for fear of the
effort and renunciation the Master said:

"How much effort and renunciation
does it take to open one's eyes and see?"

LETTING GO

"What must I do for
Enlightenment?"

"Nothing."

"Why not?"

"Because Enlightenment
doesn't come from doing
—it happens."

"Then can it never be
attained?"

"Oh yes it can."

"How?"

"Through nondoing."

"And what does one do
to attain nondoing?"

"What does one *do* to
go to sleep or to wake up?"

EXPRESSION

He was a religious writer and
interested in the Master's views.
"How does one discover God?"

Said the Master sharply, "Through
making the heart white with silent
meditation, not making paper black
with religious composition."

And, turning to his scholarly
disciples, he teasingly added, "Or
making the air thick with learned
conversation."

DISCOVERY

"Help us to find God."

"No one can help you there."

"Why not?"

"For the same reason that
no one can help the fish
to find the ocean."

WITHDRAWAL

"How shall I help the world?"

"By understanding it," said
the Master.

"And how shall I understand
it?"

"By turning away from it."

"How then shall I serve
humanity?"

"By understanding yourself."

RECEPTIVITY

"I wish to learn. Will you
teach me?"

"I do not think that you
know how to learn," said
the Master.

"Can you teach me how to learn?"

"Can you learn how to
let me teach?"

To his bewildered disciples the
Master later said: "Teaching only
takes place when learning does.
Learning only takes place when *you*
teach something to *yourself.*"

CONVERSION

To a group of his disciples whose hearts
were set on a pilgrimage the Master
said: "Take this bitter gourd along. Make
sure you dip it into all the holy rivers
and bring it into all the holy shrines."

When the disciples returned, the bitter
gourd was cooked and served as
sacramental food.

"Strange," said the Master slyly after
he had tasted it. "The holy water and
the shrines have failed to sweeten it!"

CAUSALITY

Everyone was surprised by the
Master's updated metaphor:
"Life is like a motor car."

They waited in silence, knowing
that an explanation would not
be long in coming.

"Oh yes," he said at length. "A
motor car can be used to travel
to the heights."

Another silence.

"But most people lie in front
of it, allow it to run over them,
then blame it for the accident."

COERCION

The Master demanded seriousness of
purpose from those who sought discipleship.

But he chided his disciples when
they strained themselves in spiritual
endeavor. What he proposed was
lighthearted seriousness or
serious lightheartedness—like
that of a sportsman in a game or
an actor in a play.

And much, much patience. "Forced
flowers have no fragrance," he
would say. "Forced fruit will
lose its taste."

CALCULATION

The Master would laugh at those
of his disciples who deliberated
endlessly before making up their mind.

The way he put it was: "People who
deliberate *fully* before they take a step
will spend their lives on one leg."

REVOLUTION

There were rules in the
monastery, but the Master
always warned against
the tyranny of the law.

"Obedience keeps the rules,"
he would say. "Love knows
when to break them."

IMITATION

After the Master attained Enlightenment,
he took to living simply—because he found
simple living to his taste.

He laughed at his disciples when
they took to simple living in
imitation of him.

"Of what use is it to copy my
behavior," he would say, "without
my motivation. Or to adopt my
motivation without the vision
that produced it?"

They understood him better when
he said, "Does a goat become
a rabbi because he grows a beard?"

ALONENESS

To a disciple who was always seeking
answers from him the Master said,
"You have within yourself the answer
to every question you propose—if
you only knew how to look for it."

And another day he said, "In the
land of the spirit, you cannot
walk by the light of someone
else's lamp. You want to borrow
mine. I'd rather teach you how
to make your own."

BLINKERS

"If you make me your authority,"
said the Master to a starry-eyed
disciple, "you harm yourself because
you refuse to see things for yourself."

And, after a pause, he added
gently, "You harm me too,
because you refuse to see
me as I am."

HUMILITY

To a visitor who described
himself as a seeker after
Truth the Master said, "If
what you seek is Truth,
there is one thing you must
have above all else."

"I know. An overwhelming
passion for it."

"No. An unremitting readiness
to admit you may be wrong."

REPRESSION

The Master had been on his deathbed
in a coma for weeks. One day he suddenly
opened his eyes to find his favorite
disciple there.

"You never leave my bedside, do
you?" he said softly.

"No, Master. I cannot."

"Why?"

"Because you are the light of
my life."

The Master sighed. "Have I so
dazzled you, my son, that you
still refuse to see the light
in *you?*"

EXPANSION

The Master sat in rapt
attention as the renowned
economist explained his
blueprint for development.

"Should growth be the only
consideration in an economic
theory?" he asked.

"Yes. All growth is good
in itself."

"Isn't that the thinking
of the cancer cell?" said
the Master.

ACCEPTANCE

"How can I be a great
man—like you?"

"Why be a great man?"
said the Master.
"Being a man is a great
enough achievement."

CHALLENGE

An easygoing disciple complained
that he had never experienced the
Silence that the Master frequently
commended.

Said the Master, "Silence only
comes to active people."

IRRELEVANCE

All questions at the public meeting
that day were about life beyond the grave.

The Master only laughed and did not
give a single answer.

To his disciples, who demanded to
know the reason for his evasiveness,
he later said, "Have you observed
that it is precisely those who do not
know what to do with this life who want
another that will last forever?"

"But is there life after death or is there
not?" persisted a disciple.

"Is there life before death?—that is the
question!" said the Master enigmatically.

VIOLENCE

The Master was always teaching
that guilt is an evil emotion
to be avoided like the very
devil—*all* guilt.

"But are we not to hate our
sins?" a disciple said one
day.

"When you are guilty, it is
not your sins you hate but
yourself."

75

IDEOLOGY

A group of political activists
were attempting to show the
Master how their ideology
would change the world.

The Master listened carefully.

The following day he said,
"An ideology is as good or
bad as the people who make
use of it. If a million
wolves were to organize for
justice, would they cease
to be a million wolves?"

MORALITY

The disciples would frequently be absorbed
in questions of right and wrong. Sometimes
the answer would be evident enough. Sometimes
it was elusive.

The Master, if he happened to be present
at such discussions, would take no
part in them.

Once he was confronted with this question:
"Is it right to kill someone who
seeks to kill me? Or is it wrong?"

He said, "How should I know?"

The shocked disciples answered, "Then
how would we tell right from wrong?"

The Master said, "While alive, be
dead to yourself, be totally dead.
Then act as you will and your action
will be right."

FANTASY

"What is the greatest enemy
of Enlightenment?"

"Fear."

"And where does fear come from?"

"Delusion."

"And what is delusion?"

"To think that the flowers
around you are poisonous snakes."

"How shall I attain Enlightenment?"

"Open your eyes and see."

"What?"

"That there isn't a single
snake around."

REMOTE CONTROL

To a shy disciple who wanted to become
self-confident the Master said, "You look
for certainty in the eyes of others and
you think that is self-confidence."

"Shall I give no weight to the opinion
of others, then?"

"On the contrary. Weigh everything they
say, but do not be controlled by it."

"How does one break the control?"

"How does one break a delusion?"

INVESTMENT

"How shall I rid
myself of fear?"

"How can you rid
yourself of what
you cling to?"

"You mean I actually
cling to my fears? I
cannot agree to that."

"Consider what your
fear protects you from
and you will agree! And
you will see your folly."

AWARENESS

"Is salvation obtained
through action or through
meditation?"

"Through neither. Salvation
comes from seeing."

"Seeing what?"

"That the gold necklace
you wish to acquire is
hanging round your neck.
That the snake you are so
frightened of is only a
rope on the ground."

SLEEPWALKING

The Master's expansive mood
emboldened his disciples to
say, "Tell us what you got
from Enlightenment. Did you
become divine?"

"No."

"Did you become a saint?"

"No."

"Then what did you become?"

"Awake."

DETACHMENT

It intrigued the disciples that
the Master who lived so simply
would not condemn his wealthy
followers.

"It is rare but not impossible
for someone to be rich and holy,"
he said one day.

"How?"

"When money has the effect on
his heart that the shadow of
that bamboo has on the courtyard."

The disciples turned to watch
the bamboo's shadow sweep the
courtyard without stirring a
single particle of dust.

DISTINCTION

The Master was strolling with some of his
disciples along the bank of a river.

He said, "See how the fish keep darting about
wherever they please. That's what they really enjoy."

A stranger overhearing that remark said, "How do
you know what fish enjoy? You're not a fish."

The disciples gasped at what they took
for impudence. The Master smiled at what
he recognized as a fearless spirit of inquiry.

He replied affably, "And you, my friend, how
do you know I am not a fish? You are not I."

The disciples laughed, taking this to be
a well-deserved rebuff. Only the stranger
was struck by its depth.

All day he pondered it, then came to the
monastery to say, "Maybe you are not as
different from the fish as I thought.
Or I from you."

CREATION

The Master was known to
side with the revolutionaries,
even at the risk of incurring the
displeasure of the government.

When someone asked him why he
himself did not actively plunge
into social revolution, he replied
with this enigmatic proverb:

"Sitting quietly
doing nothing.
Spring comes
and the grass grows."

PERSPECTIVE

The Master was in a mellow mood and the
disciples were inquisitive. Did he ever
feel depressed? they asked.

He did.

Wasn't it also true that he was in a
continual state of happiness? they persisted.

It was.

What was the secret? they wanted to know.

Said the Master, "This: Everything is as good
or as bad as one's opinion makes it."

SEPARATION

The Master's teachings did not
find favor with the government
that had him banished from his country.

To disciples who asked if he
never felt nostalgia the Master
said, "No."

"But it is inhuman not to miss
one's home," they protested.

To which the Master said, "You
cease to be an exile when you
discover that creation is your home."

CHANGE

The visiting historian was disposed to be argumentative.

"Do not our efforts change the course of human history?" he demanded.

"Oh yes, they do," said the Master.

"And have not our human labors changed the earth?"

"They certainly have," said the Master.

"Then why do you teach that human effort is of little consequence?"

Said the Master, "Because when the wind subsides, the leaves still fall."

RECOGNITION

As the Master grew old and infirm, the
disciples begged him not to die. Said
the Master, "If I did not go, how would
you ever see?"

"What is it we fail to see when you
are with us?" they asked.

But the Master would not say.

When the moment of his death was
near, they said, "What is it we will
see when you are gone?"

With a twinkle in his eye, the Master
said, "All I did was sit on the riverbank
handing out river water. After I'm
gone, I trust you will notice the river."

INSIGHT

The disciples were involved in a
heated discussion on the cause of
human suffering.

Some said it came from selfishness.
Others, from delusion. Yet others,
from the inability to distinguish
the real from the unreal.

When the Master was consulted, he
said, "All suffering comes from
a person's inability to sit
still and be alone."

AUTONOMY

The Master seemed quite impervious to
what people thought of him. When the
disciples asked how he had attained
this stage of inner freedom, he laughed
aloud and said, "Till I was twenty I
did not care what people thought of
me. After twenty I worried endlessly
about what my neighbors thought.
Then one day after fifty I suddenly
saw that they hardly ever thought
of me at all!"

AUTHENTICITY

The Master was never impressed by diplomas or degrees. He scrutinized the person, not the certificate.

He was once heard to say, "When you have ears to hear a bird in song, you don't need to look at its credentials."

IMMUNIZATION

To everyone's surprise the Master seemed unenthusiatic about religious education for the young.

When asked why, he said, "Innoculate them when they are young and you prevent them from catching the real thing when they grow up."

SELF-RIGHTEOUSNESS

The Master loved ordinary people
and was suspicious of those who
stood out for their holiness.

To a disciple who consulted him
on marriage he said, "Be sure
you don't marry a saint."

"Whyever not?"

"Because it is the surest way
to make yourself a martyr,"
was the Master's merry reply.

ENTHUSIASM

To the woman who complained
that riches hadn't made her
happy the Master said, "You
speak as if luxury and comfort
were ingredients of happiness;
whereas all you need to be really
happy, my dear, is something
to be enthusiastic about."

PREJUDICE

"Nothing is good or bad, but
thinking makes it so," the
Master said.

When asked to explain he said,
"A man cheerfully observed a
religious fast seven days
a week. His neighbor starved
to death on the same diet."

TOTALITARIANISM

To the disciples' embarrassment
the Master once told a bishop
that religious people have a
natural bent for cruelty.

"Why?" demanded the disciples
after the bishop had gone.

"Because they all too easily
sacrifice persons for the
advancement of a purpose,"
said the Master.

SELFLESSNESS

An affluent industrialist said
to the Master, "What do you do
for a profession?"

"Nothing," said the Master.

The industrialist laughed
scornfully. "Isn't that laziness?"

"Heavens no. Laziness is mostly
the vice of very active people."

Later the master said to his
disciples, "Do nothing and all
things will be done through you.
Doing nothing really takes a
lot of doing. Try it!"

WISDOM

It always pleased the Master
to hear people recognize
their ignorance.

"Wisdom tends to grow in
proportion to one's awareness
of one's ignorance," he claimed.

When asked for an explanation,
he said, "When you come to see
you are not as wise today as you
thought you were yesterday, you
are wiser today."

RICHES

"How would spirituality help
a man of the world like me?"
said the businessman.

"It will help you to have
more," said the Master.

"How?"

"By teaching you to desire
less."

BEATITUDE

The disconsolate stockbroker
lost a fortune and came to the
monastery in search of inner peace.
But he was too distraught to meditate.

After he had gone, the Master had
a single sentence by way of wry
comment: "Those who sleep on the
floor never fall from their beds."

LOVE

A newly married couple said,
"What shall we do to make
our love endure?"

Said the Master, "Love
other things together."

UNIVERSALITY

The Master ordinarily
dissuaded people from
living in a monastery.

"To profit from books you
don't have to live in a
library," he would say.

Or, even more forcefully,
"You can read books without
ever stepping into a library;
and practice spirituality
without ever going to a
temple."

FLOW

When it became clear that
the Master was going to
die, the disciples were
depressed.

Said the Master smilingly,
"Don't you see that death
gives loveliness to life?"

"No. We'd much rather you
never died."

"Whatever is truly alive
must die. Look at the flowers;
only plastic flowers never
die."

ADVENTURE

The theme of the Master's talk
was Life.

One day he told of meeting a pilot
who flew laborers from China into
Burma during World War II to work on
jungle roads. The flight was long and
boring, so the laborers would take to
gambling. Since they had no money to
gamble with, they gambled with their
lives—the loser jumped out of the
plane without a parachute!

"How terrible!" said the horrified
disciples.

"True," said the Master. "But it
made the game exciting."

Later in the day he said, "You never
live so fully as when you gamble with
your lives."

MORTALITY

To a disciple who begged for wisdom
the Master said, "Try this out: Close
your eyes and see yourself and every
living being thrown off the top of
a precipice. Each time you cling to
something to stop yourself from falling,
understand that it is falling too . . ."

The disciple tried it out and never
was the same again.

LIBERATION

"How shall I get liberation?"

"Find out who has bound you,"
said the Master.

The disciple returned after
a week and said, "No one has
bound me."

"Then why ask to be liberated?"

That was a moment of Enlightenment
for the disciple, who suddenly
became free.

RESTRICTION

The Master was exceedingly gracious
to university dons who visited him,
but he would never reply to their
questions or be drawn into their
theological speculations.

To his disciples, who marveled at
this, he said, "Can one talk about
the ocean to a frog in a well—or
about the divine to people who are
restricted by their concepts?"

INVOLVEMENT

The Master, while being gracious
to all his disciples, could not
conceal his preference for those
who lived in the "world"—the
married, the merchants, the
farmers—over those who lived
in the monastery.

When he was confronted about this,
he said, "Spirituality practiced
in the state of activity is
incomparably superior to that
practiced in the state of withdrawal."

NATURE

A lecturer explained how a fraction of the
enormous sums spent on arms in the modern
world would solve all the material problems
of every member of the human race.

The inevitable reaction of the disciples
after the lecture was: "But why are human
beings so stupid?"

"Because," said the Master solemnly, "people
have learned to read printed books. They have
forgotten the art of reading unprinted ones."

"Give us an example of an unprinted book."

But the Master wouldn't give one.

One day, in response to their persistence,
he said: "The songs of birds, the sounds
of insects are all trumpeting forth the
Truth. The grasses and the flowers are all
pointing out the Way. Listen! Look! That
is the way to read!"

HEAVEN

To a disciple who was obsessed with the thought of life after death the Master said, "Why waste a single moment thinking of the hereafter?"

"But is it possible not to?"

"Yes."

"How?"

"By living in heaven here and now."

"And where is this heaven?"

"In the here and now."

PRESENCE

When the disciples asked for a model
of spirituality that they could imitate,
all that the Master said was: "Hush! Listen."

And as they listened to the sounds
of the night outside the monastery,
the Master softly intoned the
celebrated haiku:

> "Of an early death
> showing no awareness
> the cicada sings."

REALIZATION

"What did Enlightenment
bring you?"

"Joy."

"And what is Joy?"

"The realization that
when everything is lost
you have only lost a toy."

TRUST

The Master would frequently assert that
holiness was less a matter of what one
did than of what one *allowed* to happen.

To a group of disciples who had difficulty
understanding that he told the following story:

> "There was once a one-legged
> dragon who said to the centipede,
> 'How do you manage all those legs?
> It is all I can do to manage one.'
>
> 'To tell you the truth,' said the centipede,
> 'I do not manage them at all.' "

NOISE

Each day the Master
would be inundated
with questions that
he would reply to
seriously, playfully,
gently, firmly.

One disciple always sat
through each session in
silence.

When someone questioned
her about it, she said,
"I hardly hear a word he
says. I am too distracted
by his Silence."

THOUGHT

"Why are you so wary of thought?"
said the philosopher. "Thought is
the one tool we have for organizing
the world."

"True. But thought can organize
the world so well that you are
no longer able to see it."

To his disciples he later said,
"A thought is a screen, not a
mirror; that is why you live in
a thought envelope, untouched
by Reality."

REVELATION

The monks of a neighboring monastery
asked the Master's help in a quarrel
that had arisen among them. They had
heard the Master say he had a technique
that was guaranteed to bring love and
harmony to any group.

On this occasion he revealed it: "Any
time you are with anyone or think of
anyone you must say to yourself: *I am
dying and this person too is dying,*
attempting the while to *experience*
the truth of the words you are saying.
If every one of you agrees to practice
this, bitterness will die out, harmony
will arise."

Having said that, he was gone.

BENEVOLENCE

A grocer came to the Master in great distress
to say that across the way from his shop they
had opened a large chain store that would drive
him out of business. His family had owned his
shop for a century—and to lose it now would
be his undoing, for there was nothing else he
was skilled at.

Said the Master, "If you fear the owner of the
chain store, you will hate him. And hatred will
be your undoing."

"What shall I do?" said the distraught grocer.

"Each morning walk out of your shop onto the
sidewalk and bless your shop, wishing it prosperity.
Then turn to face the chain store and bless it too."

"What? Bless my competitor and destroyer?"

"Any blessing you give him will rebound to
your good. Any evil you wish him will destroy you."

After six months the grocer returned to report that
he had had to close down his shop as he had feared,
but he was now in charge of the chain store and his
affairs were in better shape than ever before.

SIN

One of the disconcerting—and delightful
—teachings of the Master was: "God is
closer to sinners than to saints."

This is how he explained it: "God in heaven
holds each person by a string. When you sin,
you cut the string. Then God ties it up again,
making a knot—and thereby bringing you a
little closer to him. Again and again your
sins cut the string—and with each further knot
God keeps drawing you closer and closer."

HEALING

To a distressed person who came to
him for help the Master said, "Do
you really want a cure?"

"If I did not, would I bother to come
to you?"

"Oh yes. Most people do."

"What for?"

"Not for a cure. That's painful.
For relief."

To his disciples the Master said,
"People who want a cure, provided
they can have it without pain, are
like those who favor progress,
provided they can have it without
change."

DOCTRINE

To a visitor who claimed he had
no need to search for Truth because
he found it in the beliefs of his
religion the Master said:

"There was once a student who
never became a mathematician
because he blindly believed
the answers he found at the
back of his math textbook
—and, ironically, the answers
were correct."

BELIEF

The Master had quoted Aristotle: "In the
quest of truth, it would seem better and
indeed necessary to give up what is
dearest to us." And he substituted the
word "God" for "truth."

Later a disciple said to him, "I am
ready, in the quest for God, to give
up anything: wealth, friends, family,
country, life itself. What else can
a person give up?"

The Master calmly replied, "One's
beliefs about God."

The disciple went away sad, for he
clung to his convictions. He feared
"ignorance" more than death.

NONINSTRUCTION

"What does your Master teach?"
asked a visitor.

"Nothing," said the disciple.

"Then why does he give discourses?"

"He only points the way—he teaches
nothing."

The visitor couldn't make sense out
of this, so the disciple made it
clearer: "If the Master were to teach,
we would make beliefs out of his
teachings. The Master is not concerned
with what we believe—only with what
we see."

ORIGINS

It was the disciple's birthday.

"What do you want for a birthday
gift?" said the Master.

"Something that would bring
me Enlightenment," she said.

The Master smiled. "Tell me,
my dear," he said, "when you
were born, did you come *into*
the world like a star from the
sky or *out* of it like a leaf
from a tree?"

All day long she pondered
that strange question of
the Master. Then she suddenly
saw the answer and fell into
Enlightenment.

EXPOSURE

One day the Master asked, "What, in your opinion, is the most important of all religious questions?"

He got many answers:

"Does God exist?"

"Who is God?"

"What is the path to God?"

"Is there a life after death?"

"No," said the Master. "The most important question is: 'Who am I?'"

The disciples got some idea of what he was hinting at when they overheard him talking to a preacher:

Master: "So then, according to you, when you die your soul will be in heaven?"

Preacher: "Yes."

Master: "And your body will be in the grave?"

Preacher: "Yes."

Master: "And where, may I ask, will *you* be?"

IDENTIFICATION

"I wish to see God."

"You are looking at him
right now," said the Master.

"Then why do I not see him?"

"Why does the eye not see
itself?" said the Master.

Later the Master explained:
"As well ask a knife to cut
itself or a tooth to bite itself
as ask that God reveal himself."

COMPREHENSION

"Every word, every image used for
God is a distortion more than a
description."

"Then how does one speak of God?"

"Through Silence."

"Why, then, do you speak in words?"

At that the Master laughed uproariously.
He said, "When I speak,
you mustn't listen to the words,
my dear. Listen to the Silence."

MEANING

Said a traveler to one of the
disciples, "I have traveled a
great distance to listen to the
Master, but I find his words
quite ordinary."

"Don't listen to his words.
Listen to his message."

"How does one do that?"

"Take hold of a sontonoo that
he says. Shake it well till
all the words drop off. What
is left will set your heart
on fire."

EMPTINESS

Sometimes there would be a rush
of noisy visitors and the Silence
of the monastery would be shattered.

This would upset the disciples; not
the Master, who seemed just as content
with the noise as with the Silence.

To his protesting disciples he said
one day, "Silence is not the absence
of sound, but the absence of self."

SERVICE

The master was known to favor
action over withdrawal. But he
always insisted on "Enlightened"
action.

The disciples wanted to know
what "Enlightened" meant. Did
it mean "right-intentioned"?

"Oh no," said the Master. "Think
how right-intentioned the monkey
is when he lifts a fish from the
river to save it from the watery
grave."

BEING

"What must I do to attain
holiness?" said a traveler.

"Follow your heart," said
the Master.

That seemed to please the
traveler.

Before he left, however,
the Master said to him
in a whisper, "To follow
your heart you are going
to need a strong constitution."

APPEARANCES

The Master always frowned on
anything that seemed sensational.
"The divine," he claimed, "is only
found in the ordinary."

To a disciple who was attempting
forms of asceticism that bordered
on the bizarre the Master was
heard to say, "Holiness is a
mysterious thing: The greater it
is, the less it is noticed."

CELEBRATION

"What would spirituality give me?"
said an alcoholic to the Master.

"Nonalcoholic intoxication,"
was the answer.

HOLINESS

To a preacher who kept
saying, "We must put
God in our lives," the
Master said, "He is
already there. Our
business is to recognize
this."

FRIENDLINESS

"What shall I do to love my neighbor?"

"Stop hating yourself."

The disciple pondered those words long
and seriously and came back to say, "But I
love myself too much, for I am selfish and
self-centered. How do I get rid of that?"

"Be friendly to yourself and your self
will be contented and it will set you
free to love your neighbor."

AFFIRMATION

A woman in great distress over
the death of her son came to
the Master for comfort.

He listened to her patiently
while she poured out her
tale of woe.

Then he said softly, "I
cannot wipe away your tears,
my dear. I can only teach
you how to make them holy."

OPENNESS

An anxious couple complained
to the Master that their son had
abandoned the religious traditions
of the family and proclaimed
himself a freethinker.

Said the Master, "Not to worry.
If the lad is really thinking for
himself, the Mighty Wind is bound
to arise that will carry him to
the place where he belongs."

BONDAGE

To a fearful religious visitor
the Master said, "Why are you so
anxious?"

"Lest I fail to attain Salvation."

"And what is Salvation?"

"Moksha. Liberation. Freedom."

The Master roared with laughter
and said, "So you are *forced* to
be free? You are *bound* to be
liberated?"

At that minute the visitor relaxed
and lost his fear forever.

IMPOVERISHMENT

When a disciple came from a
faraway country, the Master
asked, "What are you seeking?"

"Enlightenment."

"You have your own treasure
house. Why do you search
outside?"

"Where is my treasure house?"

"This seeking that has come
upon you."

At that moment the disciple
was Enligthened. Years later
he would say to his friends,
"Open your own treasure house
and enjoy your treasures."

SOVEREIGNTY

The disciples sought Enlightenment,
but did not know what it was or
how it was attainable.

Said the Master, "It cannot be
attained. You cannot get hold
of it."

Seeing the disciples' downcast
look, the Master said, "Don't
be distressed. You cannot
lose it either."

And to this day the disciples
are in search of that which
can neither be lost nor taken
hold of.

WORDS

The disciples were absorbed in a discussion
of Lao-tzu's dictum:

> "Those who know do not say;
> Those who say do not know."

When the Master entered, they asked him exactly
what the words meant.

Said the Master, "Which of you knows the fragrance
of a rose?"

All of them knew.

Then he said, "Put it into words."

All of them were silent.

DISCIPLINE

To the disciples who wanted to know
what sort of meditation he practiced
each morning in the garden the Master
said, "When I look carefully, I see
the rose bush in full bloom."

"Why would one have to look *carefully*
to see the rose bush?" they asked.

"Lest one see not the rose bush,"
said the Master, "but one's preconception
of it."

MODERATION

Again and again the Master would be
seen to discourage his disciples
from depending on him, for this
would prevent them from contacting
the inner Source.

He was often heard to say, "Three
things there are that when too close
are harmful, when too far are useless
and are best kept at middle distance:
fire, the government and the guru."

CONTRADICTION

"What action shall I perform
to attain God?"

"If you wish to attain God,
there are two things you
must know. The first is that
all efforts to attain him are
of no avail."

"And the second?"

"You must act as if you did
not know the first."

EXPERIENCE

The president of a prestigious
university, convinced of the
Master's mystical experience,
wanted to make him head of
the theology department.

He approached the chief disciple
with this proposal. The disciple
said, "The Master emphasizes
being Enlightened, not teaching
Enlightenment."

"Would that prevent him from being
head of the department of theology?"

"As much as it would prevent an
elephant from being head of the
department of zoology."

PUBLICITY

There was nothing about the Master that
any but the keenest eye would see as
out of the ordinary. He could be frightened
and depressed when circumstances warranted.
He could laugh and cry and fly into a rage.
He loved a goodly meal, was not averse to
a drink or two and was even known to turn
his head at the sight of a comely woman.

When a traveler complained that the
Master was not a "holy man," a disciple
set him right:

"It is one thing that a man be holy. It
is quite another that he should seem
holy to you."

IDOLATRY

The Master never wearied of warning his
disciples about the dangers of religion.
He loved to tell the story of the prophet
who carried a flaming torch through the
streets, saying he was going to set fire
to the temple so that people would concern
themselves more with the Lord than with
the temple.

Then he would add: "Someday I shall
carry a flaming torch myself to set
fire to both the temple and the Lord!"

CULTIVATION

A traveler in quest of the divine
asked the Master how to distinguish
a true teacher from a false one when
he got back to his own land.

Said the Master, "A good teacher
offers practice; a bad one offers
theories."

"But how shall I know good practice
from bad?"

"In the same way that the farmer
knows good cultivation from bad."

TRANSIENCE

The Master had an allergy for people who
protracted their stay at the monastery.
Sooner or later each disciple would hear
the difficult words: "The time has come
for you to go. If you do not get away,
the Spirit will not come."

What was this "Spirit," one particularly
smitten disciple wished to know.

Said the Master:
        "Water remains alive and free
        by flowing.
        You will remain alive and free
        by going.
        If you do not get away from me,
        you will stagnate and die
        —and be contaminated."

NONEXPERIENCE

At a discussion on the God
experience, the Master said,
"When God is experienced,
the self disappears. So who
will do the experiencing?"

"Is the God experience, then,
a nonexperience?"

"It is like sleep," said the
Master. "The sleep experience
is only known when sleep is
over."

CONCEALMENT

The Master once told the story of a
priceless antique bowl that fetched
a fortune at a public auction. It
had been used by a tramp who ended
his days in poverty, quite unaware
of the value of the bowl with which
he begged for pennies.

When a disciple asked the Master what
the bowl stood for, the Master said,
"Your self!"

Asked to elaborate, he said, "All
your attention is focused on the
penny knowledge you collect from
books and teachers. You would do
better to pay attention to the
bowl in which you hold it."

WONDER

The Haji who lived at the outskirts of the
town was said to perform miracles, so his home
was a center of pilgrimage for large crowds of
sick people.

The Master, who was known to be quite uninterested
in the miraculous, would never reply to questions
on the Haji.

When asked point-blank why he was opposed to
miracles, he replied, "How can one be opposed
to what is taking place before one's eyes
each moment of the day?"

DECEPTION

"How shall we distinguish the true mystic from the false?" asked the disciples who had an inordinate interest in the occult.

"How do you distinguish the true sleeper from the one who is feigning sleep?" asked the Master.

"There's no way. Only the sleeper knows when he is feigning," said the disciples.

The Master smiled.

Later he said, "The feigning sleeper can delude others—he cannot delude himself. The false mystic, unfortunately, can delude both others and himself."

EVASION

A visitor narrated the story of a saint who, wanting to visit a dying friend and fearing to travel by night, said to the sun, "In the Name of God, stay on in the sky till I reach the village where my friend lies dying." And the sun stopped dead in the sky till the holy man reached the village.

The Master smiled. "Would it not have been better for the holy man to overcome his fear of traveling by night?" he said.

JUDGMENT

"How shall I forgive
others?"

"If you never condemned,
you would never need
to forgive."

LIMITATION

"Is there a God?" asked the Marxist.

"Certainly not the kind people are
thinking of," said the Master.

"Whom are you referring to when
you speak of people?"

"Everyone."

RECKLESSNESS

The Master always insisted that we must learn
by ourselves—teach ourselves—rather than
depend on other people's authority. This had
its limits, of course, as when a bright young
fellow was convinced he ought to try drugs as
a means to mysticism—and "take the risk, for
one can only learn by trial and error."

That moved the Master to tell the old story
of the nail and the screw:

> "Here is one way to find out
> whether what you need in a
> plank is a nail or a screw:
> Drive the nail in. If it
> splits the plank, you
> know you needed the screw."

INSANITY

On the question of his own Enlightenment
the Master always remained reticent, even
though the disciples tried every means to
get him to talk.

All the information they had on this
subject was what the Master once said to
his youngest son who wanted to know what
his father felt when he became Enlightened.
The answer was: "A fool."

When the boy asked why, the Master had
replied, "Well, son, it was like going
to great pains to break into a house by
climbing a ladder and smashing a window
—and realizing later that the door of
the house was open."

DEVELOPMENT

To a disciple who complained of his
limitations the Master said, "You
are limited indeed. But have you
noticed you can do things today
that you would have thought
impossible fifteen years ago?
What changed?"

"My talents changed."

"No. You changed."

"Isn't that the same thing?"

"No. You are what you think
you are. When your thinking
changed, you changed."

SHALLOWNESS

A journalist one day asked the Master to
name one thing that characterizes the
Modern World.

The Master unhesitatingly replied, "People
every day know more and more about the Cosmos
and less and less about themselves."

And to an astronomer who held him spellbound
with the wonders of modern astronomy the
Master suddenly said, "Of all the millions
of strange objects in the universe—the
black holes and quasars and pulsars—
the strangest, unquestionably, is the self!"

SURRENDER

"What is the highest act
a person can perform?"

"Sitting in meditation."

"Wouldn't that lead to inaction?"

"It *is* inaction."

"Is action, then, inferior?"

"Inaction gives life to actions.
Without it they are dead."

CREATIVITY

"What is the highest act a person
can perform?"

"Sitting in meditation."

But the Master himself was rarely
seen to sit in meditation. He was
ceaselessly engaged in housework
and fieldwork, in meeting people
and writing books. He even took
up the bookkeeping chores of the
monastery.

"Why, then, do you spend all your
time in work?"

"When one works, one need not cease
to sit in meditation."

DISAPPEARANCE

To a disciple who strained after Enlightenment
till he became physically weak the Master said,
"A ray of light can be grasped—but not with
your hands. Enlightenment can be attained—
but not by your efforts."

The puzzled disciple said, "But did you
not tell me to strive to become empty?
That is what I am attempting to do."

"So now you are *full* of effort to be
empty!" said the Master through his
laughter.

REALITY

While the Master seemed to relish life and
live it to the full, he was also known to
take great risks, as when he condemned the
tyranny of the government, thereby courting
arrest and death; and when he led a group
of his disciples to serve a plague-stricken
village.

"The wise have no fear of death," he would
say.

"Why would a man risk his life so easily?"
he was once asked.

"Why would a person care so little about
a candle being extinguished when day
has dawned?"

DISTANCE

The owner of Fun Park commented on
the irony of the fact that while the kids
had a great time at his park he himself
was habitually depressed.

"Would you rather own the park or have the
fun?" said the Master.

"I want both."

The Master made no reply.

When questioned about it later, the Master
quoted the words of a tramp to a wealthy
landowner: "You own the property. Others
enjoy the landscape."

SERENITY

"Are there ways for
gauging one's
spiritual strength?"

"Many."

"Give us one."

"Find out how often
you become disturbed
in the course of a
single day."

DEMONSTRATION

"Does God exist?" said the Master one day.

"Yes," said the disciples in chorus.

"Wrong," said the Master.

"No," said the disciples.

"Wrong again," said the Master.

"What's the answer?" asked the disciples.

"There is no answer."

"Whyever not?"

"Because there is no question," said
the Master.

Later he explained: "If you cannot *say* anything
about Him who is beyond thoughts and words, how
can you *ask* anything about Him?"

PRECEDENCE

The Master welcomed the advances of technology,
but was keenly aware of its limitations.

When an industrialist asked him what his
occupation was, he replied, "I'm in the
people industry."

"And what, pray, would that be?" said the
industrialist.

"Take yourself," said the Master. "Your
efforts produce better things; mine, better people."

To his disciples he later said, "The aim of
life is the flowering of persons. Nowadays
people seem concerned mostly with the
perfectioning of things."

INSINUATION

The Master claimed he had a book
that contained everything one
could conceivably know about God.

No one had ever seen the book
till a visiting scholar, by dint
of persistent entreaty, wrested
it from the Master. He took it
home and eagerly opened it—
only to find that every one of
its pages was blank.

"But the book says nothing,"
wailed the scholar.

"I know," said the Master
contentedly. "But see how
much it indicates!"

INFLEXIBILITY

"Heavens, how you've aged!"
exclaimed the Master after
speaking with a boyhood friend.

"One cannot help growing old,
can one?" said the friend.

"No, one cannot," agreed the
Master, "but one must avoid
becoming aged."

DESTRUCTION

For all his holiness, the Master seemed
vaguely opposed to religion. This never
ceased to puzzle the disciples who,
unlike the Master, equated religion
with spirituality.

"Religion as practiced today deals in
punishments and rewards. In other words,
it breeds fear and greed—the two things
most destructive of spirituality."

Later he added ruefully, "It is like
tackling a flood with water; or a
burning barn with fire."

OPPRESSION

The Master always left you to grow at your own pace. He was never known to "push." He explained this with the following parable:

> "A man once saw a butterfly
> struggling to emerge from
> its cocoon, too slowly
> for his taste, so he began
> to blow on it gently. The
> warmth of his breath speeded
> up the process all right. But
> what emerged was not a butterfly
> but a creature with mangled
> wings.

"In growth," the Master concluded, "you cannot speed the process up. All you can do is abort it."

FRUSTRATION

The disciples could not understand
the seemingly arbitrary manner in
which some people were accepted
for discipleship and others were
rejected.

They got a clue one day when they
heard the Master say, "Don't
attempt to teach a pig to sing.
It wastes your time—and irritates
the pig."

DEFINITIONS

The Master had a childlike fascination
for modern inventions. He could not get
over his amazement at the pocket calculator
when he saw one.

Later he said, good-naturedly, "A lot of
people seem to have those little pocket
calculators, but nothing in their pockets
worth calculating!"

Weeks later, when a visitor asked him
what he taught his disciples, he said,
"To get their priorities right. Better
have the money than calculate it; better
have the experience than define it."

DISCLOSURE

The discussion among the disciples once centered on the usefulness of reading. Some thought it was a waste of time, others disagreed.

When the Master was appealed to, he said, "Have you ever read one of those texts in which the notes scrawled in the margin by a reader prove to be as illuminating as the text itself?"

The disciples nodded in agreement.

"Life," said the Master, "is one such text."

VULNERABILITY

The Master offered the perfect solution
to a married couple that was forever
quarreling.

He said, "Just stop claiming as a
right what you can ask for as a
favor."

The quarreling instantly stopped.

OPPOSITION

To a pioneering spirit who was discouraged by frequent criticism the Master said, "Listen to the words of the critic. He reveals what your friends hide from you."

But he also said, "Do not be weighed down by what the critic says. No statue was ever erected to honor a critic. Statues are for the criticized."

INFINITY

It was impossible to get the Master
to speak of God or of things divine.
"About God," he said, "we can only
know that what we know is nothing."

One day he told of a man who
deliberated long and anxiously
before embarking on discipleship.
"He came to study under me, with
the result that he learned nothing."

Only a few of the disciples understood.
What the Master had to teach could not
be learned. Nor taught. So all one could
really learn from him was nothing.

PERSECUTION

A disciple was one day recalling how
Buddha, Jesus, and Mohammed were branded
as rebels and heretics by their contemporaries.

Said the Master, "Nobody can be said
to have attained the pinnacle of Truth
until a thousand sincere people have
denounced him for blasphemy."

AT-ONE-MENT

When a man whose marriage was in trouble sought his advice, the Master said, "You must learn to listen to your wife."

The man took this advice to heart and returned after a month to say that he had learned to listen to every word his wife was saying.

Said the Master with a smile, "Now go home and listen to every word she isn't saying."

GREATNESS

"The trouble with the world,"
said the Master with a sigh,
"is that human beings refuse
to grow up."

"When can a person be said
to have grown up?" asked a
disciple.

"On the day he does not need
to be lied to about anything."

ENLIGHTENMENT

The Master was an advocate both of learning and of Wisdom.

"Learning," he said when asked, "is gotten by reading books or listening to lectures."

"And Wisdom?"

"By reading the book that is you."

He added as an afterthought: "Not an easy task at all, for every minute of the day brings a new edition of the book!"

MANIFESTATION

When a new disciple came to the Master, this is the catechism he was usually subjected to:

"Do you know the one person who will never abandon you in the whole of your lifetime?"

"Who is it?"

"You."

"And do you know the answer to every question you may have?"

"What is it?"

"You."

"And can you guess the solution to every one of your problems?"

"I give up."

"You."

CONTEMPLATION

The Master would often say that Silence alone
brought transformation.

But no one could get him to define what
Silence was. When asked he would laugh, then
hold his forefinger up against his tightened
lips—which only increased the bewilderment
of his disciples.

One day there was a breakthrough when someone
asked, "And how is one to arrive at this
Silence that you speak of?"

The Master said something so simple that his
disciples studied his face for a sign that
he might be joking. He wasn't. He said,
"Wherever you may be, look when there is
apparently nothing to see; listen when all
is seemingly quiet."

INNOCENCE

When out on a picnic, the Master
said, "Do you want to know what
the Enlightened life is like?
Look at those birds flying over
the lake."

While everyone watched, the
Master exclaimed:

"They cast a reflection
on the water
that they have no awareness of
—and the lake has no attachment to."

ART

"Of what use is a Master?"
someone asked.

Said the disciple, "To teach
you what you have always
known, to show you what you
are always looking at."

When this confused the visitor,
the disciple exclaimed:

"An artist, by his paintings,
taught me to see the sunset.
The Master, by his teachings,
taught me to see the reality
of every moment."

SOLITUDE

"I want to be with God
in prayer."

"What you want is an
absurdity."

"Why?"

"Because whenever you are,
God is not; Whenever God is,
you are not. So how could
you be *with* God?"

Later the Master said:

"Seek aloneness. When you
are with someone else, you
are not alone. When you are
'with God,' you are not alone.
The only way to really be with
God is to be utterly alone.
Then, hopefully, God will be
and you will not."

SUSPICION

To a traveler who asked how he
could tell a true Master from a
false one the Master said shortly,
"If you are not yourself deceitful,
you will not be deceived."

To his disciples the Master later
said, "Why do seekers assume that
they themselves are honest and all
they need is a test to detect deceit
in Masters?""

PROPORTION

A visitor who was full of expectations
was unimpressed by the commonplace
words the Master addressed to him.

"I came here in quest of a Master,"
he said to a disciple. "All I find is
a human being no different from the
others."

Said the disciple, "The Master is a
shoemaker with an infinite supply of
leather. But he does the cutting and
stitching in accordance with the
dimension of your foot."

AGGRESSION

A zealous disciple expressed
a desire to teach others the
Truth and asked the Master
what he thought about this.
The Master said, "Wait."

Each year the disciple would
return with the same request
and each time the Master would
give him the same reply: "Wait."

One day he said to the Master,
"When will I be ready to teach?"

Said the Master, "When your
excessive eagerness to teach has
left you."

PRAYER

The Master never ceased to attack the notions
about God that people entertain.

"If your God comes to your rescue and gets you
out of trouble," he would say, "it is time you
started searching for the true God."

When asked to elaborate, this is the story
he told:

> "A man left a brand-new bicycle
> unattended at the marketplace
> while he went about his shopping.
>
> He only remembered the bicycle
> the following day—and rushed to the
> marketplace, expecting it would have been
> stolen. The bicycle was exactly where
> he had left it.
>
> Overwhelmed with joy, he rushed
> to a nearby temple to thank God
> for having kept his bicycle safe—
> only to find, when he got out of the
> temple, that the bicycle was gone!"

MANIPULATION

The Master sat through the
complaints a woman had
against her husband.

Finally he said, "Your
marriage would be a
happier one, my dear,
if you were a better wife."

"And how could I be that?"

"By giving up your efforts
to make him a better husband."

EXTRAVAGANCE

One day the disciples wanted to know
what sort of person was best suited
to discipleship.

Said the Master, "The kind of person
who, having only two shirts,
sells one and with the money buys
a flower."

ATTACHMENT

"I have no idea of what
tomorrow will bring, so
I wish to prepare for it."

"You fear tomorrow—not
realizing that yesterday
is just as dangerous."

EXHIBITION

When one of the disciples announced his
intention of teaching others Truth, the
Master proposed a test: "Give a discourse
that I myself shall be present at to
judge if you are ready."

The discourse was an inspiring one. At
the end of it, a beggar came up to the
speaker, who stood up and gave the man
his cloak—to the edification of the
assembly.

Later the Master said, "Your words were
full of unction, son, but you are not
yet ready."

"Why not?" said the disspirited disciple.

"For two reasons: You did not give the man
a chance to voice his need. And you are not
above impressing others with your virtue."

CONTENTMENT

Paradoxical as it seemed, the Master
always insisted that the true reformer
was one who was able to see that everything
is perfect as it is—and able to
leave it alone.

"Then why would he wish to reform
anything?" protested his disciples.

"Well, there are reformers and reformers:
One type lets action flow through them
while they themselves do nothing; these
are like people who change the shape and
flow of a river. The others generate their
own activity; they are like people who
exert themselves to make the river wetter."

GRACE

A young man came to the Master
and said, "I wish to be Wise. How
can I achieve my wish?"

The Master sighed and said, "There
was once a young man just like you.
He wished to be Wise and his wish
had great power to it. One day he
found himself sitting exactly where
I am. In front of him sat a young
man on the exact spot where you are
now. And the young man was saying,
'I wish to be Wise!' "

SUPERIORITY

An Eastern disciple who was proud
of what he considered to be the
spirituality of the East came to
the Master and said, "Why is it
that the West has material progress
and the East has spirituality?"

"Because," said the Master
laconically, "when provisions for
this world were being handed out
in the beginning, the West had
the first choice."

INCOMPETENCE

The Master would insist that the final
barrier to our attaining God
was the word and concept "God."

This so infuriated the local priest
that he came in a huff to argue
the matter out with the Master.

"But surely the word 'God' can lead
us to God?" said the priest.

"It can," said the Master calmly.

"How can something help and be
a barrier?"

Said the Master, "The donkey that
brings you to the door is not the
means by which you enter the house."

INSTRUMENTALITY

When a disciple came to take leave
of the Master so that he could return
to his family and business, he asked
for something to carry away with him.

Said the Master,
"Ponder on these things:
It is not
the fire that is hot,
but you who feel it so.

It is not
the eye that sees,
but you.

It is not
the compass that makes the circle,
but the draftsman."

COMMUNION

When it was certain that the Master was going
to die, his disciples wished to give him a
worthy funeral. The Master heard of this and
said, "With the sky and the earth for my
coffin; the sun and moon and stars for my
burial regalia; and all creation to escort
me to the grave—could I desire anything more
ceremonious and impressive?"

He asked to be left unburied, but the disciples
wouldn't hear of it, protesting that he would
be eaten by the animals and birds.

"Then make sure you place my staff near me
that I might drive them away," said the Master
with a smile.

"How would you manage that? You will be
unconscious."

"In which case it will not matter, will it,
that I be devoured by the birds and beasts."

DARING

Said a disappointed visitor,
"Why has my stay here yielded
no fruit?"

"Could it be because you lacked
the courage to shake the tree?"
said the Master benignly.

SHADOWBOXING

To newcomers the Master would
say, "Knock and the door will
be opened to you."

To some of them he would later
say conspiratorially, "How
would you expect the door to
be opened when it has never
been shut?"

FORMULATIONS

"What is it you seek?" asked the Master
of a scholar who came to him for guidance.

"Life," was the reply.

Said the Master, "If you are to live,
words must die."

When asked later what he meant, he said,
"You are lost and forlorn because you
dwell in a world of words. You feed on
words, you are satisfied with words when
what you need is substance. A menu will
not satisfy your hunger. A formula will
not slake your thirst."

UNOBTRUSIVENESS

A man of spiritual repute came to
the Master and said, "I cannot pray,
I cannot understand the Scriptures,
I cannot do the exercises that I
prescribe to others . . ."

"Then give it all up," said the Master
cheerfully.

"But how can I? I am supposed to be a
holy man and have a following in these
parts."

Later the Master said with a sigh:
"Holiness today is a name without a
reality. It is only genuine when it
is a reality without a name."

LIGHTHEARTEDNESS

In keeping with his doctrine that
nothing be taken too seriously, not
even his own teachings, the Master
loved to tell this story on himself:

"My very first disciple was so weak
that the exercises killed him. My
second disciple drove himself crazy
from his earnest practice of the
exercises I gave him. My third disciple
dulled his intellect through too much
contemplation. But the fourth managed
to keep his sanity."

"Why was that?" someone would invariably
ask.

"Possibly because he was the only one
who refused to do the exercises." The
Master's words would be drowned in
howls of laughter.

VANITY

The Master frequently reminded his disciples that holiness, like beauty, is only genuine when unselfconscious. He loved to quote the verse:

> "She blooms because she blooms,
> the Rose:
> Does not ask why,
> nor does she preen herself
> to catch my eye."

And the saying: "A saint is a saint until he knows that he is one."

EDUCATION

Suspicious as the Master was of knowledge
and learning in matters divine, he never
missed a chance to encourage the arts and
sciences and every other form of learning.
So it was no surprise that he readily accepted
an invitation to address the university convocation.

He arrived an hour ahead of time to wander
about the campus and marvel at the facilities
for learning that were quite nonexistent in
his own day.

Typically, his convocation speech lasted
less than a minute. He said:

> "Laboratories and libraries,
> halls and porch and arch
> and learned lectures—
> all shall be of no avail
> if the wise heart
> and the seeing eye
> are absent."

TRIBULATION

"Calamities can bring growth and Enlightenment," said the Master.

And he explained it thus:

> "Each day a bird would shelter in the
> withered branches of a tree that stood
> in the middle of a vast deserted plain.
> One day a whirlwind uprooted the tree,
> forcing the poor bird to fly a hundred
> miles in search of shelter—till it finally
> came to a forest of fruit-laden trees."

And he concluded: "If the withered tree had survived, nothing would have induced the bird to give up its security and fly."

FEARLESSNESS

"What is love?"

"The total absence of fear,"
said the Master.

"What is it we fear?"

"Love," said the Master.

MAYA

This is how the Master once explained the
fact that Enlightenment came not through
effort but through understanding:

"Imagine all of you are hypnotized to
believe there is a tiger in this room.
In your fear you will try to escape it,
to fight it, to protect yourselves from
it, to placate it. But once the spell
is broken there is nothing to be done.
And you are all radically changed:

So understanding breaks the spell,
the broken spell brings change,
change leads to inaction,
inaction is power:
You can do anything on earth,
for it is no longer you who do it."

PURIFICATION

The Master insisted that what he taught
was nothing, what he did was nothing.

His disciples gradually discovered that
Wisdom comes to those who learn nothing,
unlearn everything.

That transformation is the
consequence not of something
done but of something dropped.

GENIUS

A writer arrived at the monastery
to write a book about the Master.

"People say you are a genius.
Are you?" he asked.

"You might say so," said the
Master, none too modestly.

"And what makes one a genius?"

"The ability to recognize."

"Recognize what?"

"The butterfly in a caterpillar;
the eagle in an egg; the saint
in a selfish human being."

HUMANITY

Much advance publicity was made for the
address the Master would deliver on
"The Destruction of the World" and a
large crowd gathered at the monastery
grounds to hear him.

The address was over in less than a minute.
All he said was:

"These things
will destroy the human race:
politics without principle,
progress without compassion,
wealth without work,
learning without silence,
religion without fearlessness
and worship without awareness."

REJECTION

"What kind of a person does Enlightenment
produce?"

Said the Master:

"To be public-spirited and belong to no party,
to move without being bound to any given course,
to take things as they come,
have no remorse for the past,
no anxiety for the future,
to move when pushed,
to come when dragged,
to be like a mighty gale,
like a feather in the wind,
like weeds floating on a river,
like a mill stone meekly grinding,
to love all creation equally
as heaven and earth are equal to all
—such is the product of Enlightenment."

On hearing these words, one of the younger
disciples cried, "This sort of teaching is not
for the living but for the dead," and walked
away, never to return.

INDEX OF SUBJECTS